**Other books by this author:**

*To Be Invisible: Unveiling the Truth about Eating Disorders*

*Understanding Autism and Positive Behavioural Support*

*Level 3 Diploma for Children and Young People's Workforce: A comprehensive learner support guide*

*Dementia Care Certificate Levels 2 & 3*

*Leadership and Management in Health and Social Care and Children and Young Peoples' Services – The down-to-earth learner support guide*

*Dedicated to Amina and Timmy*

# Understanding Autism

# and

# Positive Behavioural Support

*A Handbook and Teaching Resource*

S.K. Porter-Brooks

# Contents

# Chapter 1 – What is Autism?

Autism comes from the Greek word 'autos', which means 'self'. The term itself, however, has not always meant what it means to us today.

Our understanding of the condition, autism, has developed slowly, in conjunction with developments in research and understanding in areas of mental health and psychology.

Here is a short timeline to show how our understanding of autism has changed and developed through history:

| | |
|---|---|
| 1887 | Dr John Langdon Down outlined a definition for Down's syndrome. Named after him, Down's syndrome is caused by the presence of all or part of an extra 21st chromosome.  |
| | He also researched about mental retardation, although his description of what he meant by 'developmental retardation', would today have included those on the autistic spectrum. [i] |
| | In 1868, Dr Langdon founded the Normansfield Hospital, which was continued by his sons after he died. The hospital was closed in 1997: however, the building is still home to the Langdon Down Museum of Learning Disability, and the headquarters of the Down's Syndrome Association. [ii] |

| 1911 | The psychiatrist from Zurich, Eugen Bleuler initiated the use of the word autism, to describe some symptoms of schizophrenia. |
| | |
| | He was also in favour of eugenics, stating for example that 'the more severely burdened, should not propagate themselves...' |
| | |
| 1927 | Eugene Minkowski, who was a student of Bleuler, extended Bleuler's depiction of autism as the 'trouble generator' of schizophrenia. |

1943

In the United States, Leo Kanner developed research focussing on individuals with emotional and behavioural difficulties and linked the symptoms to a condition that he termed 'Early Infantile Autism'.

At a similar time, Hans Asperger in 1944 in Germany, also conducted similar research, and coined the term 'Asperger's syndrome' for individuals that exhibited symptoms that he outlined.

It became clear, that while the symptoms described by both Kanner and Asperger were similar, they were also different.

Asperger's syndrome was characterised by a similar difficulty in terms of social interactions, but they also had stronger language ability, and had an above average understanding of highly technical knowledge. [iii]

| 1940s-50s | Kanner put forward the idea that children with autism are more likely to originate from highly intellectual families, especially where the style of the mother was 'cold' or 'distant'. This led to the term 'refrigerator mother' developing. |
|---|---|
| | The idea was further postulated in the 1950s by Bruno Bettelheim, who believed that autism was an emotional disorder caused by infliction of physical harm on to them by their mothers. |
| | These theories were later discredited: however, they have been blamed for decades of upset and unnecessary blame being accorded to mothers of autistic children. Unfortunately, the myth of the 'refrigerator mother' syndrome, still exists today. |
| 1964 | Bernard Rimland argued for the first time, that autism was a biological condition, and not related to the parent-child bond, and he founded the Autism Society of America. |

| | |
|---|---|
| 1970s | Eric Schoper began the TEACCH programme, or the Treatment and Education of Autistic and Related Communication Handicapped Children programme at the University of North Carolina. |
| 1977 | Susan Folstein and Michael Rutter produced a research study involving a cohort of 21 same-sexed twin pairs, where either one or both twins showed symptoms of infantile autism. They reached the conclusion that brain injury sustained in the womb or during birth, could result in autism, or together with a combination of genetic predisposition. |

| 1980 | Autism was added, under the term 'infantile autism', to the *Diagnostic and Statistical Manual of Mental Disorders – Third Edition (DSM-III)*. This step improved the consistency of diagnosis of autism, and differentiation from other conditions such as schizophrenia. |
| --- | --- |
| 1987 | The term 'Infantile autism' was replaced by the term 'Autistic Disorder'. |
| 1994 | Both PDD-NOS (Pervasive Developmental Disorder – Not Otherwise Specified) and Asperger's Syndrome, were added to the Diagnostic and Statistical Manual of Mental Disorders – Fourth Edition (DSM-IV) |

**ACTIVITY**

Watch the following video clip, entitled 'Heroism: Refrigerator Moms and Autism', by Kartemquin (approx. 4 mins):

https://www.youtube.com/watch?v=WWB_OYWE3DQ

Questions:

- What effect did the 'Refrigerator Mom' theory, have on the mother of the autistic son, in the clip?

- What might have been the long-term effect on her, as well as her family?

**REFLECTION ACTIVITY**

- Is there still potential for confusion between autism and mental health conditions, like schizophrenia?
- Is it possible for people to have more than one diagnosis?

## *The Characteristics of Autism*

Children with autism are all unique. The condition manifests itself in different levels of severity and in very unique and individual ways. In turn, some aspects of the condition can become more distinct, as a child matures, but may be confused or misinterpreted in the early stages.

The phrase 'Triad of Impairment' is used to encapsulate the array of symptoms that autism brings, which can be categorised into three main areas: impairment in social communication; impairment in imagination and impairment in social relationships.

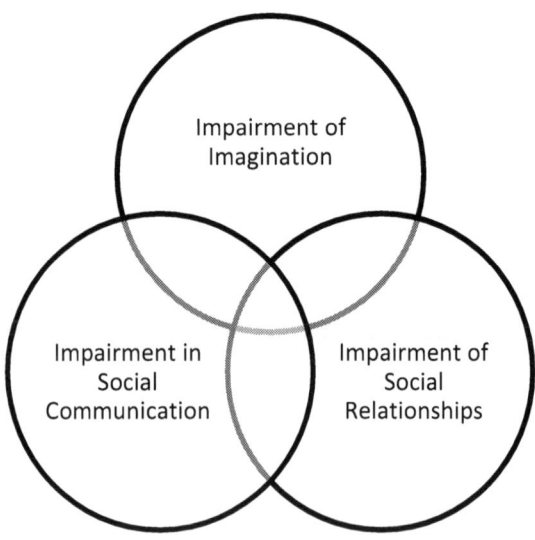

**Figure 1 Triad of Impairment characterising ASD**

## *Impairment in social communication*

Impairment in social communication, can manifest itself in the form of a difficulty in being able to communicate effectively with other people. In practice, this might be because they struggle to read between the lines of what people mean, or to understand nuances of speech. They may struggle to generate rapport, to relay a sense of empathy during conversation. For example, they might ask repetitive questions, or talk about their own interests, regardless of the listener's response. They may appear to communicate only to meet their own needs, rather than to engage socially. At times, they may also make factual comments, that appear inappropriate to the topic of conversation at hand.

Even at the early stages of development, children with autism may exhibit delays in key developmental milestones: they struggle to 'babble' or develop early sounds or gestures for communicating needs. Sometimes, babies may show initial babbling sounds, but then lose these communicative behaviours as they grow older.

Most individuals with autism can develop spoken language with support despite varying length of delay. However, some children and adults remain nonverbal or nearly non-verbal. Some individuals may learn to use other types of communication systems: such as pictures, sign language, or speech-generating devices.

Sometimes individuals may develop some spoken language but will not use it in conventional ways. They may repeat the same word or words repeatedly. Or they may repeat what others say, a tendency known as echolalia.

At other times, some individuals may develop impressive communication skills, and yet at the same time may struggle with other aspects of communication, such as sustaining a conversation, or understanding the subtle social cues that operate during a conversation between two or more people.

Difficulties in interpreting body language can also impact on communication. Autistic individuals can struggle to interpret and understand body language or gestures of others. Likewise, they may struggle to exhibit appropriate body language, or indeed any cues such as facial expressions or gestures, in a way that matches what they are saying.

Often a young person with autism may resort to challenging behaviour or show frustrations, which are essentially signs that they need help to express themselves. With the right kind and level of support to help the person express themselves, then the challenges raised by behavioural matters naturally tend to reduce.

## *Impairment in Imagination*

The second area that can encapsulate symptoms of autism, can be described as 'impairment in imagination'. During a child's development, a child can often be observed being engaged in imaginative play.

This might include play activities like 'trying on Mum's shoes', dressing up in costumes or role-playing. An autistic child may, however, display varying levels of difficulty with imaginative play. They may display difficulty in flexible thinking in terms of interests, routines, perspectives and rules. They may struggle to understand other people's points of view or feelings. They may interpret everything in literal terms: for example, use of the phrase 'keep your eyes peeled' would be interpreted literally. They may display a preference for clear, structured, predictable routines: and become disturbed or agitated if there are sudden changes to a routine.

Another very common symptom of autism, is the display of repetitive behaviours, or a tendency to focus on a restricted range of activities. An individual may exhibit such behaviour as rocking, fidgeting, getting up and down or producing repetitive sounds or words.

They also may develop a tendency to only engage in a very limited range of activities, such as putting toys in a row, or developing an obsessive interest in rigid routines, or particular topics.

## *Impairment in Social Relationships*

The third area relates to impairment in social relationships. The phrase 'social relationships', relates to not just our relationships with family and close friends, but acquaintances that we make through the course of daily activities (e.g. when we go into a shop, or speak to the postman), or meet someone for the first time (e.g. on the bus; or when starting a new class in school).

Individuals with autism often display difficulties in understanding how to behave and interact with other people. These difficulties may include non-verbal forms of communication (e.g. eye contact; gestures; facial expression); body positioning; understanding of personal space or boundaries).

They may express or exhibit an intense desire to have friends and relationships but struggle to understand the social mores and conventions to initiate and maintain friendships and relationships.

The recurrent experience of obstacles in forming relationships, rejection or failure, can lead to individuals with autism isolating themselves from social contact, which exacerbates and intensifies their sense of social insecurity and anxiety even further.

From an early age, children with autism may exhibit symptoms, such as difficulties engaging in give-and-take that characterise daily interactions with others. From as early as 8-10 months, a child may not respond when their name is called or may exhibit delayed speech or sound. Toddlers with autism, may struggle to interact with their peers, or play social games or imitate others, and exhibit a preference to play alone. They may struggle to react in expected patterns, when a parent shows displays of emotion, whether anger or affection.

Individuals with autism do experience strong attachment to their parents. Because of their difficulties in expressing and interpreting other peoples' thinking and feelings, however, some of the social cues that are so important within relationships and communication, can be lost. They may struggle to interpret a smile or wave rapidly enough, or at all.

They may also struggle with trying to understand other people's thoughts, or to empathise with others.

Furthermore, they may find it difficult to regulate their emotions, and at times display sudden or inappropriate behaviour, such as crying, being disruptive or physically aggressive at inappropriate times. At times, this kind of behaviour may result from underlying frustration or anxiety, and can translate into self-injurious behaviour, or self-harming.

## *Other characteristics of Autism*

The symptoms are by no means restricted to those three categories, but they form a useful framework for understanding the commonality of symptoms that all individuals on the autistic spectrum share, to a lesser or greater degree. Individuals can also experience other areas of difficulty as well, however. These might relate to sensory difficulties, mood disorder or attention problems.

Associated neurological issues that some autistic individuals can experience include mood disorders (e.g. anxiety; depression; bipolar syndrome), sleep problems, attention deficit, immune dysfunction or gastrointestinal disorders. As well as these, some individuals may also experience additional related disorders, such as Obsessive-Compulsive Disorder (OCD), Attention Deficit Hyperactivity Disorder (ADHD) or Intellectual Disability.

**Associated systemic issues and other related disorders**

- Sleep disorders
- Mood disorders
- Anxiety disorders
- OCD
- ADHD
- Intellectual disability

**Associated neurological issue**

- Sleep deficits
- Mood
- Anxiety
- Hyperactivity
- Attention difficulties
- Immune dysfunction
- Gastro-intestinal Disorders
- Seizures

**Core Autism Symptoms**

- Social deficits
- Repetitive behavoiurs
- Language impairment

**Figure 2 Other conditions often coexistent with ASD**

**Table 1 Core Symptoms of Autism**

| | |
|---|---|
| **Impairment in imagination** | Deficits in flexible thinking regarding interests, routines, perspectives and rules. |
| | Does not understand other people's points of view or feelings. |
| | Agitated by changes in routine. |
| | Cannot generalise information |
| | Has special interests |
| | Takes everything literally |
| **Impairment in social relationships** | Deficits in understanding how to behave and interact with other people |
| | Inappropriate touching of other people |

| | |
|---|---|
| | Difficulty understanding and using non-verbal behaviour, e.g. eye contact, facial expression, gestures. |
| | Stands too close to people |
| | Unaware of the different ways to interact with friends, staff and strangers. |
| | Has desire to have friendships and relationships, but struggles to initiate and maintain them. |
| **Impairment in social communication** | Deficits in ability to communicate effectively with other people |
| | Asks repetitive questions |
| | Cannot read between the lines of what people mean. |
| | Talks about own interest regardless of the listener's response. |

| | |
|---|---|
| | Makes factual comments inappropriate to the context. |
| | Absence of desire to communicate. |
| | Communicates for own needs, rather than for 'social' engagement. |
| **Additional difficulties** | Sensory difficulties, mental health & physical difficulties etc. |
| | Cannot bear loud noises |
| | Maybe hyper or hypo sensitive to touch, clothes or pressure. |
| | Mood disturbances, e.g. anxiety, aggression, or depression. |
| | Motor difficulties, e.g. walking on tip-toes, clumsiness. |
| | Attention difficulties |

## Associated Medical Conditions

### Genetic Disorder

There are several identifiable genetic conditions that affect some individuals with autism. These include:

- Fragile X syndrome
- Angelman syndrome
- Tuberous sclerosis
- Chromosome 15 duplication syndrome
- Other single-gene or chromosomal disorders

Single cell disorders are thought to be an underlying cause for 15-20% of autism diagnoses.

### Seizure Disorders

It is thought that approximately 39% of individuals with autism, also have a seizure disorder, such as epilepsy. Individuals with an intellectual disability as well, appear to have a greater propensity to have epilepsy as well.

## Sleep Dysfunction

Sleep problems are common in children and adults with autism. They may find it hard to get to sleep, or experience waking in the night, or poor quality of sleep. These difficulties can also often impact on other behavioural, cognitive and emotional functioning in the day time.

## Sensory Processing Problems

Many children and adults with autism may either experience hyposensitivity or hypersensitivity to sensations such as sounds or touch. An individual who is hypersensitive might feel uncomfortable wearing heavy clothing or being touched. An individual, who is hyposensitive, may struggle with processing of sounds or other sensory stimuli, such as smells or light.

## Pica

Sometimes individuals with autism may fail to move on from a tendency in infancy to put non-food items in their mouth, and this can prevail or exacerbate, with items like dirt, clay, chalk or paint chips being picked up to be put in the mouth.

## Sensory Differences

Individuals with autism can often experience either 'hypersensitivity' or hyposensitivity. We will be looking at the different manifestations of this phenomenon, and at the impact that this condition can have on an individual's life as well.

### Sensory Overload

An individual with autism can sometimes feel that too many sensory stimuli, such as noise, crowdedness, bright lights, quickly overpowering. Individuals will have different thresholds, and different triggers.

The range of sensory difficulties that can be experienced as a result of autism, is explored in more detail in the following table:

**Table 2 Sensory Effects of Autism**

| Sight | |
|---|---|
| **Under-Sensitive** | **Over-sensitive** |
| - Objects can appear darker and indistinct<br>- They may have stronger peripheral vision compared to central vision<br>- Objects in peripheral vision may be blurred, and objects in central vision be greatly magnified<br>- Lack of depth perception, with resulting difficulties in matters like throwing or catching. | - Objects may appear to move or jump around in one's vision<br>- Objects may appear broken up or fragmented<br>- Individuals may tend to focus on details of an object, rather than the object as a whole<br>- Sensitivity to light, may cause difficulties in getting to sleep |
| **Ways to help:** Consider using visual supports or coloured lenses | Consider making adaptations to the environment: e.g. blackout curtains; not using bright lights indoors; providing sunglasses. |

| Sound | | |
|---|---|---|
| **Under-Sensitive** | | **Over-sensitive** |
| - Individuals may have partial hearing loss in one ear or both<br>- They may not react or respond to particular sounds<br>- They may prefer areas with loud noises, or which are crowded | | - May perceive noises louder than they really are<br>- Sounds may be blurred and difficult to hear clearly<br>- May be able to hear sounds a long way in the distance<br>- They may have difficulty concentrating, and find it difficult to cut out environmental sounds or background noise (e.g. television on the background) |
| **Ways to help:** | Find ways to back up verbal information: e.g. via pictorial cues/ TEACCH. Ensure | Try to minimise background or environmental noises by: shutting doors or windows; providing ear plugs; |

| sufficient sensory stimulation is embedded in the daily schedule, or timetable. | planning well before going to a crowded place. |
| --- | --- |

| Smell | |
| --- | --- |
| **Under-Sensitive** | **Over-sensitive** |
| - May not be able to detect smells at all, including own body odour<br>- May use other sensory processes to compensate for lack of smell: e.g. licking an object to identify what it is. | - Smells may be perceived in an overpowering way<br>- They may have fears which result during toileting<br>- May respond negatively to people with strong smelling perfumes, cigarette smoke or shampoos |
| **Ways to help:** You could support them with regular washing routines; use strong- | Avoid using strong-smelling perfumes or shampoos etc. |

| | smelling personal hygiene products | |
|---|---|---|

| Taste | |
|---|---|
| **Under-Sensitive** | **Over-sensitive** |
| - May have a preference to strong tasting or spicy food<br>- Pica – may put non-edible items into mouth (e.g. stones; dirt, soil; metal; grass; faeces) | - May have a limited diet, as certain tastes may be perceived as overpowering<br>- May have a preference for certain textures of food: e.g. ice-cream. |
| **Ways to help:** | Encourage a varied diet as much as possible, within their taste/ food preferences |

| Touch | |
|---|---|
| **Under-Sensitive** | **Over-sensitive** |
| - May have limited sensation when touching something: may clutch something for a long | - May find touch painful or unpleasant.<br>- May become restless or fidgety if anything is on the hands or feet |

| | | |
|---|---|---|
| | time, to allow time for the sensation to 'process'<br>- May have a high threshold for pain<br>- May not notice food in the mouth<br>- May engage in self-harming behaviours<br>- May smear faeces<br>- May enjoy heavy blankets at night time in bed<br>- May put things in the mouth frequently: e.g. clothing | - May not like having hair brushed<br>- May not like certain textures of food<br>- May not tolerate certain textures in fabric or clothing |
| **Ways to help:** | Consider providing alternative textured items for the individual to hold, to distract from smearing: e.g. jelly/ cornflour and water. For chewing, consider providing straws/ or hard sweets for them to | Tell them before you are about to touch them; do not hug them if they find it painful; adjust texture of food that they can tolerate; introduce new or different textures slowly; don't rush them when doing something they find uncomfortable (e.g. brushing teeth); providing |

| | |
|---|---|
| chew instead of objects. | clothing of a texture that they can tolerate. |

| Balance | |
|---|---|
| **Under-Sensitive** | **Over-sensitive** |
| - May rock, swing or spin in a repetitive motion or manner | - May find certain sports difficult, where there is a need to control movements: e.g. swimming.<br>- May feel car sick frequently<br>- May struggle in certain activities where the head isn't upright, and the feet are off the ground<br>- May have difficulty during an activity, where they have to stop quickly. |

| Ways to help: | Consider supporting them to do activities that help develop their vestibular system: e.g. swings, rocking horses, roundabouts, seesaws, catching, walking up steps or down curbs. | Break tasks down into manageable steps, and provide visual cues. |
|---|---|---|

| Body awareness | |
|---|---|
| **Under-Sensitive** | **Over-sensitive** |
| - May stand too close to other people; may lack appreciation of personal space<br>- May find it difficult to move between rooms and around furniture<br>- May accidentally bump into people frequently | - May have poor fine motor skills, and find some activities difficult: e.g. tying shoe laces or doing up buttons<br>- Turns the whole body to look at something |

| | | |
|---|---|---|
| **Ways to help:** | Consider avoiding placing furniture in the middle of the room, but to the side instead. You could provide weighted blankets at night time. Use coloured tape to create distinctive borders between rooms or areas. | You could provide activities that help develop someone's find motor skills: e.g. artistic activities; lacing; beading |

| Synthaesthesia |
|---|
| This condition, which is also very rare, is where a person receives sensory input through sensory system, and out through another. For example, when they hear a sound, they could experience it as a colour. |
| iv |

## *Language and Intellectual Ability Variations*

Children on the autistic spectrum may receive a further specific diagnosis of Asperger Syndrome/ High Functioning Autism or Classic Autism. These conditions tend to be differentiated by language ability.

Children with Asperger Syndrome/ High Functioning Autism may have IQs that fall within the normal, or even the superior range; they also have more advanced early development of language.

It is important not to generalise, however, as there is also a lot of differentiation between Asperger Syndrome, and high functioning autism, which do not exactly correlate, and within the group sometimes referred to as having 'low functioning' autism.

In the medical field, diagnoses are made based on the degree to which symptoms have an impact on daily 'functioning': high functioning, is where an individual has good expressive speech, fair to good receptive understanding, and fair ability to function independently in their daily settings. The term, 'low functioning' is used to refer to individuals who have very limited verbal skills and are often non-verbal. They may also have lower intellectual abilities, and extreme difficulty understanding daily instructions, and need significant degrees of assistance in doing daily activities. [v]

However, level of functioning does not always correlate with severity of autism. Sometimes children who are labelled 'high functioning' may have severe autistic traits: e.g. very rigid/ inflexible thinking, very resistant to change and uncertainty, and meltdown over slight changes to their routine. On the other hand, some children who are considered 'low functioning' because they are nonverbal, may have difficulty performing personal care, but have less severe autistic traits: for example, they may be more flexible in their thinking, handle daily transitions more easily, relate better to others, and have fewer meltdowns.

It is important not to equate 'lack of verbal skills' with low intellectual abilities. There are many children who are non-verbal but have higher cognitive abilities than one might at first expect. They may need assistance to communicate in adaptive ways. We must always assume that an individual has the 'competence' or ability to learn, without making initial assumptions, and not rely too much on 'low versus high functioning' labels.[vi]

## *Impact on the lives of individuals and those around them*

Siblings and family members can be tremendously affected in a family with a child with Autistic Spectrum Disorder. Sometimes a sibling can feel and experience a tremendous amount of closeness and concern for a child with ASD. However, there are also other factors that can increase the risk of other additional behavioural and emotional difficulties experienced by siblings.

Support provided for a child with autism, should be directed as support for the family as a whole. Siblings should also be allowed to express themselves in their own way, and to be heard. Siblings may often be surrounded by lots of well-meaning parents and professionals, advocating on behalf of them, and the child with ASD, however they may at times be not given sufficient opportunity to express a voice of their own.[vii]

Here is an outline of some of the effects on siblings, of having a child in the family with ASD:

| Alleviating Factors | Potential Additional Pressures |
|---|---|
| They may feel able to appreciate one's siblings as unique and different. | Siblings may have traits of autism themselves as well, possibly undiagnosed. |
| They may have others to talk to with similar experiences. | The sibling relationship may feel 'different' from other sibling relationships. |
| They may experience positive parent-child interactions. | They may experience having parents with mental health problems; or experience a tense pressured environment within the family home. |
| Parents may receive sufficient support for mental health problems, and the family may develop a stronger bond with each other as they develop resilience to negotiate the difficulties together. | |

Here are some quotes of siblings' experiences of growing up in a family with a child with ASD, from a report conducted by Michael Petalas, Professor R. Hastings, Dr S Nash and Dr A. Dowey, of Bangor University in 2009:

*Lizzy – I like that he always shows who he is. He always shows that he does have a personality and he is someone. And also just so he can't talk doesn't mean he doesn't have anything to say. He can sort of speak to you in a way.*

*Maddie – (....) it would be nice to have a nice, normal brother because I could do more with him, so that would be better.*

*Leah – when like you play with something, Jack he comes along because he wants to put it in a little order; and he absolutely takes it off you. And say you just walk off and just go and sit in the sitting room and go and watch TV, he just comes in and starts chucking things at you, (...) he just chucks things at you, shouts at you, screams at you'*

## *Social and Cultural Diversity*

### *Gender*

It is now increasingly recognised, that it is harder to both recognise and diagnose autism in girls. Traditionally, Autism has been seen to be a condition that predominantly affects boys, and four times as many boys as girls are diagnosed.

A study carried out by the SSC, Simons Simplex Collection, found that 'among individuals with autism who have an intelligence quotient (IQ) lower than 70, girls have greater social communication impairments than do boys...Girls in this group also have lower IQs on average than the boys do'.[viii]

The study also found that the girls within the study group also demonstrated more irritability and externalizing behaviours, than boys who had the disorder.

It has been proposed that girls who do receive a diagnosis of autism, will be much more severely affected than males, as more genetic mutations are required to produce autism in females.

Compounding the diagnostic difficulties, sometimes girls may demonstrate more 'stereotypical restricted interests' that can more easily evade notice, than autistic boys' restricted interests. For example, an autistic girl may develop a restricted interest in a pop singer, whereas a boy might develop one about train timetables: the latter is more likely to raise attention.

Some have suggested that we need gender-specific ways of diagnosing autism and girls, as traits such as restricted interests or social skills vary so greatly according to gender. Examining girls with autism using boy-centric criteria, could prevent certain symptoms being picked up. In some cases, girls with autism may be misdiagnosed, as solely having a social communication disorder, or intellectual disability alone, and then miss out on other potentially beneficial behavioural interventions.

## Ethnicity and culture

### *Service provision, health inequalities and stigma*

A number of studies have been conducted, which have highlighted the relationship between service provision and stigma towards autism. This is often because, when there are more effective services, then individuals with autism and their family or carers, are able to access community services and live more freely with a greater level of independence and openness. greater

A study by Grinker et al (2011), revealed that communities displayed greater understanding and awareness of autism, where there were broader and more effective autism service provisions.[ix]

It follows that health inequalities, and unequal access to services, has a knock-on effect to real and perceived stigma. A study by the Kings Fund in 2015, found that some BME communities faced poorer access to all healthcare service: partly due to language barriers, but also cultural misunderstandings or unease[x]. For example, sometimes people from BME communities interpret the phrase 'independent living' as meaning leaving g the loved ones who need looking after, to live on their own: when in fact, 'independent living' is a broadly defined vision, that is shaped by personal, family and other contextual circumstances. In addition, sometimes, minority groups have poor experiences from service providers, and then reject them. This can result in carers become more isolated, financially insecure, and under pressure.

Religion is also an important aspect of culture, and there has been empirical research conducted which has revealed a greater tendency to stigmatise people with mental illness, in highly religious communities. The may partly because, in areas where healthcare services are poor, people revert or rely more on religion to explain, support or provide comfort for difficulties faced by families affected by disability of any form.

A study by Bankole (2016), found that in some African cultures, autism is believed to be a result of witchcraft or poor parenting.[xi] Another study by Alqahtani (2012), argued that some in parents in Saudi Arabia attributed the cause of autism to the 'evil eye' bestowed on them, in unfortunate circumstances. [xii]

## *Effects of Stereotyping and Discrimination*

Stereotyping can be broadly broken down into three main forms:

- Negative attitudes: e.g. authoritarianism
- Negative knowledge: e.g. misconceptions
- Negative behaviours: e.g. avoidance[xiii]

The impact of stereotyping and discrimination is immense and long-term. Here are some examples:

### *Employment stigma and discrimination*

According to research conducted by Redman et al (2009), only 15% of autistic adults in the UK were in full-time employment, even though 79% of those on incapacity benefit say they would like to work.

## Social and emotional loneliness

The Bancroft et al (2012) report showed that nearly a quarter of all autistic adults reported having no friend at all, while nearly two thirds, reported their main friend being their family or carer.

## Hate crime

A project known as the 'Living in Fear' project, conducted in 2014, found that nearly half of those individuals with autism interviewed, had experienced some form of victimisation.

## Mate crime

Individuals with autism are particularly vulnerable to being befriended by others, who go one to utilise that friendship to manipulate or bully them. Children and adults with autism are also at extra risk of experiencing online bullying.

## Mental health problems

Individuals with autism are more at risk of experiencing mental health problems, such as depression and self-harm.

In cultural contexts where there are fewer services provided for autistic people, there is likely to be a greater prevalence of stigma, and a lower understanding in general about autism.

## Collectivist cultures

Some have argued that certain 'collectivist cultures' are more likely to produce conditions where individuals with autism and/or their families are more likely to feel victimised or afraid to come forward. Papadopoulos et al, 2013 has argued that 'collectivist cultures (which place priority on community interdependence and shared group norms and values) are generally more likely than individualist cultures (which place priority on personal independence, goals and values) to stigmatise people who deviate from the norm'.

## Health inequalities

Families, who are caring for an individual with autism, may experience poor cultural awareness from service providers, which can lead to them under-utilise or reject services altogether. Poorer access to healthcare can be also compounded by language barriers as well.

## *Religion*

In communities where there is a higher level of religious faith, there may also be a poorer availability of services, or a greater level of mistrust towards services, due to poor cultural awareness conveyed by them. This can consequently lead to poorer understanding of autism. Autism is frequently conceptualised in African cultures, as resulting from witchcraft or poor parenting, while in some Middle Eastern cultures, they may understand autism as having arisen as a result of the 'evil eye'.

*Theories about autism related to: brain function and genetics; psychology*

There is still a lot unknown about the causes of autism, and other autism spectrum disorders.

In very rare cases, it is thought autism may be linked with certain agents that can cause birth defects, however it is thought that genetic factors have a predominant influence on the causality of autism.

Other causes have been suggested and proposed in the past, although scientific evidence is patchy at best.

| Genetics | It is thought, based on more recent studies of twins, that the hereditability of autism spectrum disorders, is approximately 60-90%. |
| --- | --- |
| | Despite the evidence of strong heritability, most cases of ASD occur sporadically, without any evidence of recent family history of ASD. It is |

| | thought that these cases are possibly a result of *de novo* mutations, in the sperm or mother's egg.

The mutations themselves however, can result in considerable variation of individual outcome, and nature of autistic traits resulting. |
|---|---|
| **Prenatal environment** | Advanced age of either parent; diabetes; bleeding; use of psychiatric drugs by the mother during pregnancy. |
| **Infection** | Rubella or cytomegalovirus |
| **Environmental factors** | Exposure of the embryo to: e.g. valproic acid, paracetamol, thalidomide, misoprostol; alcohol

While it is possible that autism could be initiated or affected later in pregnancy, there is a lot of evidence to suggest that it arises early on during development. |

| Other maternal conditions | Thyroxine deficiency<br>Diabetes |
|---|---|
| Perinatal environment | Low birth weight; long gestation duration<br>Hypoxia during childbirth |
| Postnatal environment | Amygdala neurons: problems with the development of the area of the brain (the amygdala) that governs social perception, has been suggested to have a possible causal relationship with autism. |
| Autoimmune disease | Some scientists have suggested that autism may be caused as a result of an individual's own antibodies, perhaps due to an environmental trigger after birth, such as an infection, although such a theory is controversial. |
| Endogenous opiate precursor theory | In 1979, Jaak Panksepp investigated a possible link between autistic children with autism, and a possible digestive disorder from birth, that had caused conversion of gluten (wheat-based |

| | |
|---|---|
| | foods) and casein (present in dairy products) into opioid compounds, which interfered with neurological development.<br><br>The possibility of a relationship between consumption of gluten and casein, and autism, was further investigated by Kalle Reichelt in 1991, although the scientific evidence is still not comprehensive. |
| **Gastrointestinal factors** | Some parents have described gastrointestinal (GI) disturbances in autistic children, although the results are still inconclusive. |
| **Lack of Vitamin D** | Some scientists have suggested Vitamin D deficiency may play a role in causing autism, although not a lot of research has been conducted yet. |
| **Lead** | Some scientists have reported that blood levels of autistic children may |

| | be higher than typical levels, although it is hard to determine if this might be a cause or consequence of autism. |
|---|---|
| **Refrigerator mother** | Bruno Bettelheim popularised, a now largely refuted theory, that lack of maternal warmth during early childhood, was a causal factor behind autism. |
| **Vaccines** | In 1998, Andrew Wakefield *et al.*, reported a study of 12 children who had autism and bowel symptoms, and who had in some cases demonstrated their symptoms after the MMR vaccine. His research study was later discovered to be fraud and a manipulation of data, however, and the findings retracted. |

## Sources of Support and Advice

The experience of looking after an individual with autism is a very unique one, and will vary vastly from one family, and one situation, to the next.

Some broad ideas, advice and links to external sources of advice, have been compiled in the table below, however:

| Parents and carers | <ul><li>Support about getting a diagnosis</li><li>Education advice: Education Rights Service</li><li>Employment advice</li><li>Family support services: e.g. EarlyBird and EarlyBird Plus</li><li>Short breaks and befriending schemes</li><li>Care and benefits</li><li>Advice about benefits, community care and housing issues for older adults on the autistic spectrum</li><li>Research into autism and Asperger's syndrome.</li></ul> |
|---|---|

| | |
|---|---|
| **Partners** | - Expand your own knowledge about autism and Asperger's syndrome |
| | - Read accounts of other partners of autistic people |
| | - Try not to get too emotional when talking about any problems in your relationships. |
| | - You could write down any issues that are arising, but: use clear language; only write about one issue at a time; focus about solutions to the problem, not just 'the problem'; encourage their input and their suggestions; give them time to think about it. |
| | - Avoid personal criticism: don't say 'You mustn't do this'. Instead, say, 'people don't do this….' |
| | - Talk about concrete rather than abstract concepts: try not to pressurise them to over-analyse or interpret their own/ or your thoughts or feelings. |
| | - The Autism Helpline, provide a database of counsellors, who can |

| | |
|---|---|
| | support individuals and partners on the autistic spectrum.<br>- Don't assume that a partner can understand your nonverbal cues, e.g. when you need a hug or some affection. You may need to express your wishes and emotions more openly.<br>- You may find drawing up visual timetables, or visual reminders, can help you manage household matters together.<br>- Seek advice from a counsellor for relaxation techniques. |
| | Other links:<br>- NAS Autism Helpline: 0808 800 4104<br>- Asperger Syndrome Foundation: www.aspergerfoundation.org.uk<br>- Different Together (an online community for partners of people affected by Asperger syndrome): www.different-together.co.uk<br>- Disability, Pregnancy and Parenthood International – (a charity that supports parents with |

| | |
|---|---|
| | disabilities, their families and professionals): www.dppi.org.uk / 0800 018 4730 (Tuesday and Thursday 10:30am to 3:00pm) |
| **Grand-parents** | - Broaden your own knowledge about autism, by visiting National Autistic Website*(correct)<br>- Be aware of other siblings' needs as well: give them opportunity to share time with you as well, or let them store some special possessions at your house, if they are afraid of and sibling potentially breaking them<br>- Support the parents/ and autistic child to maintain existing established routines, and introduce changes gradually<br>- Consider issues such as sensory overload, or sensory impairment in your grandchild, and adapt the environment or surroundings, to help them manage more easily<br>- Attend Autism Seminars for Families, along with your son or daughter |

| | |
|---|---|
| | - Investigate any local support groups or activities<br>- The website, Grandparents Plus, supports grandparents who have lost contact with their grandchildren or have a caring role in their grandchild's life. |

## *Differences in Terminology for ASD*

As our understanding about autism has gradually increased since the theory of 'Refrigerator Mothers' was prevalent, so has the sense of empowerment and awareness of rights amongst individuals with autism and their carers.

Cultural acceptability of different terminology has also been influenced by this trend, as there has been a gradual shift towards more positive and assertive language. Often the terms we use can have a wider affect, in terms of changing attitudes towards individuals with autism, which can improve their own experiences and opportunities for inclusion.

Terms such as 'on the autism spectrum' and 'Asperger syndrome', are on the whole regarded as acceptable. Autistic adults also seem to prefer identity-first terminology, like 'autistic', or 'Aspie'. Professionals also commonly use the term 'autism spectrum disorder'.

There are at times differences of opinion between groups though. Families tend to be less likely to like terms such as

'Aspie'. Other terms, like 'low functioning', 'Kanner's autism' and 'classic autism' are also disliked.[xiv]

## *Contribution of Autism Rights Groups*

The Autism Rights Movement, sometimes abbreviated to ARM, has fought for autistic people to be recognised as neurologically diverse, and not 'deficient' or 'wanting'.

The movement has been influenced and is interlinked to some extent with broader movements for disability rights and neurodiversity.

The main focus of the autism rights movement, is to spread the proactive message of acceptance of autistic behaviours, and to promote the use of therapies that help autistic individuals themselves to cope with their neurological difficulties, rather than therapies aimed at making them look or appear like their 'neurotypical peers'.

The movement also sees autism as being a natural expression of human genes, and not a result of a genetic 'defect' (the mainstream perspective), or environmental factors (e.g. pollution or vaccines).

See below, for a timeline showing the background to this movement:

## Brief Timeline about Autism Rights Movements

| 1962 | The National Autistic Society was set up, with assistance from Lorna Wing as one of its founders, to improve the lives of individuals with autism and Asperger's syndrome. |
|---|---|
| 1980s | Jim Sinclair co-founded the Autism Network International and communicated the anti-cure or autism rights perspective. |
| 2004 | Michelle Dawson challenged the ethics behind Applied Behaviour Analysis (ABA). Aspies for Freedom (AFF) was also founded. |
| 2006 | The Autism Acceptance Project was founded by Estee Klar in the USA. |
| 2008 | The Autistic Self Advocacy Network (ASAN) succeeded in halting two advertisement campaigns that it felt were demeaning to autistics. |

## *Controversies concerning the search for cures and interventions for autistic spectrum conditions and for pre-natal diagnosis*

Some of the concerns and perspectives that autism activists, as well as family members of autistic individuals, find most concerning – and at times gruelling, are as follows:

-   That autism is similar to a condition like 'cancer', only that it lasts for an entire life
-   That children with autism are 'held hostage to a psychiatric disorder'.
-   Terms used, such as 'mad child disease'.
-   That the increase in prevalence and diagnoses of autism can be described as an 'epidemic', as autism is akin to other 'diseases'
-   Some have tried to determine the 'financial cost of autism': though activists, such as Michelle Dawson, point out that no effort has been made to examine the cost of 'eliminating the disease' to autistic individuals.

In contrast to some of those views and perspectives, autistic activists and advocates argue that:

- Autistic individuals have got their own culture, just as other people might have their own religion or background.
- Autistic individuals themselves should be present at parent- and professional-led organisations and conferences that relate to autism, and have their own views and voices heard.
- Amanda Baggs has argued that there are many autistic people, who are intelligent and articular, who may also experience self-harming behaviours and need support with personal care. Baggs has mentioned an example of an autistic individual, who had services withdrawn, as it was discovered that they could type.
- Aspies For Freedom have raised concerns about the ethical basis behind many common therapies. For example, AFF has argued that ABA therapy aims to reduce or extinguish behaviours like stimming, or to force eye contact and break routines. They argue that

behaviours such as stimming, are in fact an autistic person's way of communicating.

- There is also opposition to prenatal genetic testing of autism in the womb, and the prevention of autistic people being born.
- There has also been much opposition to the notion of a cure for autism. Activists argue that autism is a characteristic or a trait, and not a disease that needs to be cured.

Simon Baron-Cohen, a Profession of Developmental Psychology at Trinity College, Cambridge, has expressed that:

'I do think there is a benefit in trying to help people with autism-spectrum conditions with areas of difficulty such as emotion recognition. Nobody would dispute the place for interventions that alleviate areas of difficulty, while leaving the areas of strength untouched. But to talk about a 'cure for autism' is a sledge-hammer approach and the fear would be that in the process of alleviating the areas of difficulty, the qualities that are special – such as the remarkable attention to detail, and the ability to concentrate for long periods on a small topic in depth – would be lost. Autism is both a disability and a difference. We need to find ways of alleviating the disability while respecting and valuing the difference.'

On the other hand, some people argue vehemently in support of finding a cure. Here is a summary of some of the arguments from the pro-cure perspective:

-   Treatment or pursuit of a cure, will reduce autistic peoples suffering, and supports autistic children through the transition to adulthood.
-   They argue that denying children from relevant treatment, such as ABA, is also unethical.
-   Some argue that those activists who campaign against cures, are more likely to be high functioning autistic, or have Asperger's Syndrome.
-   Sue Rubin, author of *Autism Is A World,* argues that individuals with low functioning autism have a severe disability, that affects every aspect of daily life, and the need and craving for treatment and cure is extreme

# Chapter 2: What is Challenging Behaviour?

At times, some individuals with autism may display behaviour that is potential harmful to themselves or others around them, and one may describe such behaviours as 'challenging behaviour'. Examples of such behaviour are wide-ranging however, and unique to each individual and their situation.

For example:

- Physical aggression: hitting; pushing; poking; throwing objects at someone; punching
- Verbal aggression: shouting; swearing; insulting others
- Damage to property: breaking own possessions (even items that are special to them); damage to buildings/ fascia/ equipment
- Self-stimulation: rocking; putting objects in mouth; masturbation; talking to oneself
- Lack of concern for others: pushing in front of other people; saying hurtful comments to others
- Withdrawal: refusal to interact with others

- Self-harming: head-banging; cutting; pulling hair; ingesting objects or dangerous substances; placing ligatures around neck

*Why does Challenging Behaviour take place?*

As children develop in their infancy, particularly when they still have early communication skills and abilities, they will often display challenging behaviour, especially during the period commonly known as 'the terrible twos'. For example, if a two-year-old is tired, but still wants to play with their toys or their friends, they might begin to cry or get angry. This is because at an early stage in development, children do not yet have well developed social or communication skills and are not able to communicate what they want in more sophisticated ways, which emerges later on as their communication improves. [xv]

Children with autism or learning disabilities, however, may take even longer to develop communication and social skills to help them communicate their needs, and so behavioural responses that help them communicate a need or elicit a response, can become embedded or more difficult to adjust.

Children with autism or learning disability, as we have seen, may have additional difficulties which compound or increase their communication difficulties: for example, sensory impairment or epilepsy.

As their developmental pathways may be different, children with autism and learning disability, when they do find themselves exposed to settings or situations (e.g. school; being in public places) may be less well equipped to cope with them, and so challenging behaviour helps them to escape from situations where they feel uncomfortable or unsafe.

In the past, and at times still to this day, sometimes the response to people who display challenging behaviour, has been to restrict them in institutional settings, and to deprive them of social contact or interactions with the wider community. In these situations, compounded by communication difficulties, the risk of abuse increases exponentially, which of course exacerbates the confidence, wellbeing and behaviour of these vulnerable people even more.

In extension to this analysis, if challenging behaviour has just arisen, or if it appears to be worsening, then it is important to consider if there is a biological or emotional reason behind it.

In the table below, is a list of examples of different reasons behind challenging behaviour:

| Difficulty communicating a need or concern |
| --- |
| Stress, depression or anxiety |
| Environment stimuli: e.g. unfamiliar people or noises; too hot or too cold |
| Reactions to staff: e.g. unfamiliar staff; commands; use of complicated language; lack of attention given to service user |
| Reactions to parents, friends or relatives |
| Physical illness: e.g. ear ache; constipation; heart-burn; nausea; headache; toothache |
| Feeling low in self-esteem or confidence |
| Hypo/ hyperglycaemic episode accompanying diabetes |
| Hypothyroidism: caused by insufficient thyroid hormone being produced (common in people with Down's syndrome), resulting in fatigue, constipation and depression. |
| Premenstrual tension; other hormonal changes; puberty |
| Boredom |

## Responding to challenging behaviour

The most important factors needed in addressing challenging behaviour are: time, teamwork and patience. Challenging behaviour is not something that can be cured with a pill. There is, however, a lot that can be done, with patience and perseverance.

## Ways to prevent challenging behaviour:

- Seek ways to alleviate or address any underlying medical conditions, or sensory impairment.
- Ensure that the service user is supported to have their everyday needs met, when they need it: e.g. assistance with practical activities; attention; fluid and nutrition; interesting and preferred activities etc.
- Support service users to develop their communication skills, confidence and independence, so they have the skills or ability to make choices, make decisions or communicate their wishes, rather than providing them things 'on a plate' all the time. If a person doesn't have any way of exerting control over their lives in this way, they will struggle to cope

in situations where they need to 'fend for themselves' or 'speak up for themselves' to some extent.

*Early intervention*

- If it hasn't been possible to prevent challenging behaviour, then early intervention is the next best thing.
- Address the behaviour as an indication of a possible previously undetected problem. Is there a medical issue or emotional difficulty?
- Trial and error: does stopping or changing something, stop the behaviour? Can you find a way to teach the child or person how to communicate what they want, without resorting to the behaviour?
- Keep a track record of when the behaviour occurs, and what you have tried already to address it.
- ***Only*** ignore the behaviour if it is safe to do so (that they are in a safe situation, and are able to cope if the behaviour continues)

## The Five Stages of Emotional Arousal

When a service user is upset or angry about something, their emotions intensify and then go through a journey that is called 'the five stages of emotional arousal'.

1. *Triggering*: this is the stage where the behaviour has been sparked or triggered.
2. *Build*-up: at this stage, the behaviour is intensifying, and they are becoming more agitated, anxious or erratic in behaviour. They may also behave unpredictably.
3. *Crisis*: at this point, the service user has lost control and the challenging behaviour is at its highest.
4. *Recovery:* the service user has begun to show signs of calming down: e.g. breathing more slowly.
5. *Post-crisis depression:* the service user may feel embarrassed, ashamed, depressed, mistrustful of staff, and may not want to talk to anyone or show signs of withdrawal.

## What should you do?

At the trigger and build-up stage, you should respond in accordance with the primary behavioural strategies, that should be outlined in the service user's care plan. This might include verbal reassurance; changing activity; diverting the service user's attention to something else; supporting them to go to a quieter or more familiar environment. You should use open body language, and talk reassuring, and listen to what the service user is trying to tell you. These strategies may be effective in preventing the behaviour from escalating further.

When a service user is at crisis in regard to their behavioural control, it is important that you adhere to the guidelines in their care plan, and not respond in a way that could exacerbate the situation even more. You should ensure that you have an adequate staffing ratio, and have a safe level of support, from staff with appropriate level of training and experience. You should try to diffuse the situation by distracting the service user, changing the activity, as described above. You should also maintain normal eye contact, but do not stare, and show concerns and empathy for the service user. Do not shout, but talk in a calm tone and at a low pitch. Display empathy and a willingness to listen to the person, and encourage them to communicate their concern. You should keep your hands at a waist height, and have open hand gestures, to show a non-confrontational poise, and also stand sideways on, so that you can move out quickly if you need to and avoid danger.

During the recovery phase, you need to offer lots of reassurance, and find activities that the service user enjoys doing, to help them maintain their emotions and behavioural control on a positive path. Try to avoid the trigger that started the episode, or any other triggers sparking anther behavioural incident.

During the post-crisis phase, you should follow the service user's care plan, which should outline if the person prefers to be left alone at this time, or to be supported or talk about what has happened. They might like to have a conversation about what happened and to help them rebuild trust with their support staff.

## Reactive and Proactive Responses to Challenging Behaviour

The interventions that are used during the 'trigger' and early stages of a behavioural incident, are often much milder and supportive, than interventions that are utilised during the crisis stage. Moreover, the more stressful and upsetting the crisis stage, and staff responses to it, the longer and more protracted the recovery and post-crisis phase, with increased risk of the trigger of the original behaviour remerging again.

Reactive responses are interventions that are used during or after an individual is at a crisis level in terms of their behavioural control. They are often more unpleasant and more distressing than proactive responses.

## Restraint

Restraint can often mean physical restraint, but there are other means of restraint. For example, restraint can occur by removing an individual's walking aid, use of sedatives, locking of doors or preventing access to an area.

There are strict guidelines over the use of restraint. The Mental Capacity Act 2005 stipulates that restraint can only be used if it necessary to protect the person from harm and is proportionate to the risk of harm.

In turn, the guidance published by the Care Quality Commission states that:

> Restraint is illegal unless it can be demonstrated that for an individual in particular circumstances not being restrained would conflict with the duty of care of the service. And that the outcome for the individual would be harm to themselves or for others.

## What you must NEVER do when responding to challenging behaviour

- Punish the person by withholding necessities or services: e.g. food, drink, medication, clothes or bedding; access to doctors, dentists or hospital appointments.
- Use medication to control behaviour, unless agreed and approved by a multidisciplinary team and GP.
- Forcibly seclude a person: e.g. lock doors; putting cot sides up or positioning furniture in such a way that a service user cannot get out.
- Tie service users to furniture, or use straps on wheelchairs etc, so the person has restricted movements
- Use psychological abuse: e.g. threats
- Remove devices needed by people with disabilities or sensory impairments: e.g. hearing aids; glasses; walking aids.

- Use inappropriate use of surveillance that invades a person's privacy, and undermines their dignity: e.g. pressure pads by doors[xvi]

*If you witness any of the above happening, or it is reported to you, you should follow your in-house safeguarding policies and procedures.*

**ACTIVITY**

- Think of ways staff may inadvertently use 'restraint' in the workplace, when supporting individuals with autism.

- How do you think the use of restraint can be reduced in care settings for individuals with autism?

# Chapter 3: Positive Behavioural Support

Positive Behavioural Support is an evidence-based approach towards supporting individuals who exhibit challenging behaviour, because of a broad array of external or internal stimuli or conditions.

In essence, PBS is an evidence-based theory and adaptive based methodology, to help identify ways to support individuals with challenging behaviour, and to support them in a way that reduces or minimises the risk of challenging behaviour.

It is an evidence-based approach, that is embedded in proactive practice-based leadership and collaborative team-work.

To explore the notion of 'evidence', read the scenarios on the following page:

*Reflection Exercise*

**TASK 1**

How do you think you should respond to the following examples of challenging behaviour, based on the nature and amount of information you are given in the scenarios below:

SCENARIO 1:

*You have arrived on shift, and you are told that patient 'X' hit a member of staff, 'Y', yesterday.*

SCENARIO 2:

*You observe a member of staff talking abruptly to a colleague, who is supporting a service user in the lounge. The first member of staff is rebuking the colleague for not helping the service user put on clean trousers that morning. As the staff member walks away from the lounge, the service user begins to hit his head with his hands, and say 'I don't want to get changed! I don't want to get changed!'*

# TASK 2

## SCENARIO 1:

*A member of staff during the handover meeting reports that a service user had been 'whining' and 'just wanted attention', and advised staff to be firm and not to respond too quickly to all his requests, as they were fuelling his attention seeking.*

## SCENARIO 2:

*A staff member comes to you in your office, and informs you that they are very concerned with how a staff member has spoken to another patient. They report that the staff member told the patient to 'SIT DOWN!', in a loud commanding voice, and that the person looked evidently scared and intimidated. Later on that day, other members of staff report that the patient in question has been very challenging all day, shouting at staff and telling them to leave him alone.*

After reading the scenarios above, reflect on the following questions:

- Why is it dangerous to make assumptions about the reasons behind a person's challenging behaviour?
- Why is evidence gained from direct observation sometimes better than indirect reporting?
- Why is it important not to rush in coming to a hypothesis that explains a person's challenging behaviour?

## *Key Areas of Positive Behavioural Support*

There are ten concepts that underpin Positive Behavioural Support.

These will be looked at in detail in the following section, but have been grouped into three main areas:

| |
|---|
| **VALUES** |
| PERSON-CENTRED APPROACHES |
| **THEORETICAL APPROACHES** |
| APPLIED BEHAVIOURAL ANALYSIS |
| SPEECH AND LANGUAGE THERAPY |
| COGNITVE BEHAVIOURAL THERAPY |
| OCCUPATIONAL THERAPY |
| **PROCESS** |
| SPELL FRAMEWORK |
| ACTIVE SUPPORT |

## *Values*

Values should influence and guide the way individuals with behavioural challenges are supported, and how decisions are made. Very often, these values can be seen as 'optional', when in fact they are intrinsic to the Code of Conduct for health and social care workers, and as such compulsory and regulated by internal and external quality assurance mechanisms.

Six values are now recognised as applying to health and social care workers. These are known as 'The 6 Cs', which refer to the following:

- Care: this means having a person-centred focus on the needs and best interests on the individual needing supporting, bearing in mind their holistic needs as a person to promote their mental and physical wellbeing.
- Compassion: this embraces a number of skills and aptitudes, such as being open-minded and willing to get to know and learn about a person's background, personality or interests; willing and able to use and

adapt communication techniques to be able to foster a positive rapport; being able to develop empathy and 'put yourself in someone else's shoes'

- Competence: this includes having the theoretical underpinning knowledge, that is required to carry out the job (e.g. induction training; accredited or specific training; regular updates), and to be able to translate this into practical application within the work role.
- Communication: skills in communication are essential in health and social care, because it is fundamental to developing positive rapports with service users, working as a team, and ensuring consistent and effective records are kept.
- Courage: this means having the confidence and integrity to speak out when you think something isn't right, if you want to make a suggestion, or challenge an opinion in a professional manner.
- Commitment: this is about being able to maintain and show a dedication and commitment to matters like punctuality, honesty and attention to your work responsibilities over and above your personal commitments or priorities.

Challenging behaviour can invoke intense feelings of stress and anxiety on the part of care-givers, especially if the cause of the challenging behaviour is unclear, or if it is particularly prolonged or frightening. Having a clear focus on values, can help to ensure that after an episode of challenging people, that all care-givers involved in the episode can analyse the incident from the advantage of emotional distance and clarity, and to consider all the factors that had been involved, impartially and fairly.

Values can also steer the thinking of care-givers to make sure they are focussed on the underpinning processes that support people with behavioural challenges the most: e.g. how to promote better communication; how to build more trusting and more lasting rapport; how to improve competence and develop compassion and empathy. Without values, responses to challenging behaviour will quickly drift far from the principles of Positive Behavioural Support, and become more about punishing the person, and reacting to crises, rather than proactively. [xvii]

Watch the following video to gain an introduction to the concepts of PBS: https://youtu.be/WNuW3Xqnjws

# Theoretical Approaches

| Applied Behavioural Analysis | Applied Behaviour Analysis (ABA) is an evidence-based therapeutic intervention and is based on the science of learning and behaviour. |
| --- | --- |
| | The underlying aim of ABA is to reduce harmful behaviours that are harmful to the person or others, or affect learning and development. |
| | ABA therapy programmes work towards this goal, by developing strategies that increase a person's language or communication skills, or improve attention, memory or social skills. |
| | ABA can be used in most settings: e.g. home; school; community. The approach can involve either one-to-one teaching and support, or group support. |
| | A core part of ABA is positive reinforcement, which involves using |

interventions that aim to reinforce desired behaviour, and reduce the problematic behaviour[xviii].

The framework of ABC observation charts is utilised to help focus intervention on the target behaviour.

Antecedent relates to factors that are occurring before the target behaviour (e.g. a verbal prompt, such as a request or command; a physical stimulus, such as a noise, or an object in the environment; an environmental influence or internal trigger (e.g. a feeling or thought)

The target behaviour: e.g. response to the antecedent (e.g. withdrawal; reaction; verbal or physical response)

Consequence: (e.g. what follows the behaviour; positive reinforcement of a positive behavioural response you are trying to maintain; or no reaction to inappropriate behavioural responses)

EXAMPLE:

Antecedent: The care practitioner says "We need to put away the toys now" at the end of the day.
Behaviour: The student yells "no!" and throws toys.
Consequence: The care practitioner takes away the toys and says "Okay, toys done."

How ABA would seek to reinforce a better behavioural response in this example:

Antecedent: The care practitioner says "it's time to put the toys away now" at the end of the day.

Behaviour: The student is reminded to ask, "Can I have 5 more minutes?"

Consequence: The care practitioner says, "Of course you can have 5 more minutes!"

| | |
|---|---|
| **Speech and Language Therapy (SALT)** | Nearly 1:5 of the population will experience communication difficulties, of some kind, at some point in their lives.<br><br>SALT can help people of all age groups and situations. For example:<br><br>Infants: SALT can help babies who were born prematurely, or infants who are affected by conditions like cerebral palsy, cleft palate or Down syndrome. SALT can assist address a wide range of difficulties from drinking, swallowing or play/ communication skills.<br><br>Children: SALT can help children experiencing primary speech and language difficulties, such as stammering. SALT can also help to address communication difficulties that are secondary to other issues, such as learning difficulties or hearing impairments. |

| | |
|---|---|
| | Adults with learning difficulties: SALT can support adults with diagnosed developmental disorders, such as learning disabilities, Down syndrome or Autistic Spectrum Disorder.<br><br>Adults: SALT can also help adults, who can experience communication and/or swallowing problems later in life, due to medical conditions such as stroke, cancer, head injury, Parkinson's disease or dementia.[xix] |
| **Cognitive Behavioural Therapy (CBT)** | Cognitive Behavioural Therapy can be an effective way to support and treat people with a wide range of mental health conditions. These conditions can include: obsessive compulsive disorder (OCD); panic disorder; post-traumatic stress disorder (PTSD); post-traumatic stress disorder (PTSD); phobias; eating disorders; sleep disorders or problems; other long-term physical health |

| | |
|---|---|
| | problems - e.g. irritable bowel syndrome or chronic fatigue syndrome.

The therapy is focussed on looking at the interconnections between thoughts, feelings, physical sensations and actions, as well as negative thoughts that are difficult to escape from or negate.

CBT aims to look at the negative patterns that affect how a person feels, and addresses the need for coping mechanisms to deal with current problems, rather than focussing on past issues. |
| **Occupational Therapy** | Occupational therapy is about the use of professional assessment and planned intervention to help support individuals to maintain, develop or recover their ability to engage in meaningful activities or occupations.

OTs support all sorts of people with care needs, and age groups: such as people |

| | with mental health difficulties, disabilities, injuries or other kinds of impairments (e.g. sensory). |
|---|---|

## *Process*

PBS is about using a clear and rational methodology.

No change to someone's behavioural support plan should be made without facts and evidence. No PBS plan should be based on opinions or guesswork.

A formal assessment, based on ABC charts or functional behavioural assessments should be made before a PBS plan, or amendments to it are made.

PBS plans should have a long-term focus for improving the quality of life for that individual. It isn't about 'quick fixes'.

The templates on the following pages show the stages that are involved in implementing Positive Behavioural Support, and the management processes that underpin them.

Your organisation may have slightly different ways of working, or ways of capturing the information in these forms.

## ABC Charts/ Observation Form

These forms or charts are used by healthcare practitioners to record primary observational records following an episode of challenging behaviour.

Time: What time did the behaviour occur? How long did the episode last?

Antecedent: What was the individual doing prior to the episode of challenging behaviour? What was the context behind the behaviour? Were there any environmental factors? What had the individual been doing beforehand? Were there other staff or service users present?

Behaviour: What happened? Try to be as detailed as possible.

Consequences: What happened after? Did they stop the activity? Did they go somewhere quieter to reduce sensory overload? (Do not focus on what the staff's reactive response was, although this is relevant. E.g. their outing was postponed, and they had to go to their room. The service user stopped playing the activity that was frustrating him, and after the behavioural episode became subdued and went to his room where he stayed for several hours.)

| Functional Behavioural Assessment Observation Form | | | |
|---|---|---|---|
| Individual's Name: | | Date: | |
| Staff name: | | Observer: | |
| Activity being undertaken: | | Other relevant information: | |
| **Time (e.g. start-finish; or duration)** | **Antecedent** | **Behaviour** | **Consequences** |
| | | | |

**Task Analysis:** Task Analysis is for determining where assistance is required, and in what form, to maximise independence and potential.

| Task Analysis: Example | |
|---|---|
| **Description of the task: Making toast** | |
| **Fewer, larger steps** | **More smaller steps** |
| 1. Get bread out | 1. Open bread bin |
| | 2. Pick up packet of bread |
| | 3. Put bread on table |
| | 4. Open packet and take out one slice. |
| 2. Put bread in toaster | 5. Put bread into toaster |
| 3. Switch toaster on and set dial | 6. Switch toaster on and set dial |
| 4. Start toaster | 7. Press lever down on toaster |
| 5. Get plate | 8. Open cupboard |
| 6. Get butter and jam | 9. Pick up plate out of cupboard |
| | 10. Close cupboard door. |
| | 11. Put plate on table |
| | 12. Open fridge |
| | 13. Pick up butter and put on table |
| | 14. Pick up jam and put on table |
| | 15. Close fridge |
| 7. Get knife and spoon. | 16. Open drawer |
| | 17. Pick up knife and put on table |
| | 18. Pick up spoon and put on table |
| | etc. ... |

## Participation Record

This is used for helping to assess the level of the individual's participation in different areas of independent living.

| Participation Record (example) | | | | | | | | | |
|---|---|---|---|---|---|---|---|---|---|
| **Name:** | | | | | | | | | |
| **Activity:** | Sun | Mon | Tue | Wed | Thur | Fri | Sat | Sun | Total |
| Self-care | | | | | | | | | |
| Meals | | | | | | | | | |
| Clearing up after meals | | | | | | | | | |
| Tidying and cleaning | | | | | | | | | |
| Laundry | | | | | | | | | |
| Shopping | | | | | | | | | |
| Gardening & DIY | | | | | | | | | |
| Home Leisure | | | | | | | | | |
| Family and friends | | | | | | | | | |
| Community activities | | | | | | | | | |

# Participation Summary & Staff Engagement Observation Form

This is utilised by management to help capture an overview, which can then be analysed to determine areas where an individual is enjoying better or less participation in different types of activities. The findings can then be used to reassess the support that is being given in different areas, and to identify areas for improvement.

This form on the following page can used as a template to observe staff interacting with service users, and to record and provide constructive feedback about the quality of engagement.

| Week Commencing: | Self-care | Meals | Clear after meals | Tidy and clean | Laundry | Shopping | Gardening and DIY | Home leisure | Family and friends | Community activities | Total |
|---|---|---|---|---|---|---|---|---|---|---|---|
|  |  |  |  |  |  |  |  |  |  |  |  |
|  |  |  |  |  |  |  |  |  |  |  |  |
|  |  |  |  |  |  |  |  |  |  |  |  |
|  |  |  |  |  |  |  |  |  |  |  |  |
|  |  |  |  |  |  |  |  |  |  |  |  |
|  |  |  |  |  |  |  |  |  |  |  |  |

## Staff Engagement Observation Form

| Name of unit: | | Name of staff observing and assessing: | |
|---|---|---|---|
| Date of observation: | | Time/ Duration: | |
| Number of service users supported present: | | Service user initials: | |
| Number of staff present: | | Staff initials: | |

*In the section below, give a brief description of what the person and the staff were doing/ saying during the activity you observed. After the observation, make sure you give constructive feedback.*

| Activity of the service user/s being supported: | |
|---|---|
| What were the staff doing: | |

| | 1 | 2 | 3 | 4 | 5 | Additional feedback: |
|---|---|---|---|---|---|---|
| Service users are engaged in meaningful activities and relationships, and are supported to develop independence, choice and social inclusion. | | | | | | |
| Service users are supported to participate in a range of valued activities. | | | | | | |
| Service users are offered choices and their decisions are respected appropriately. | | | | | | |
| Activities are presented well. | | | | | | |
| Activities are prepared well. | | | | | | |
| Service users are supported with graded assistance to successfully participate in meaningful activities and relationships. | | | | | | |
| Service users are supported in a positive, compassionate and helpful manner. | | | | | | |
| Rating scale: 1 = very weak (urgent need for improvement); 2 = weak (inconsistent, poor performance, could be improved); 3 = adequate; 4 = good (many strong points, consistent good performance); 5 = excellent (outstanding, hard to do better than this) | | | | | | |

## *SPELL Framework*

The National Autistic Society's SPELL framework, is designed to help people on the autistic spectrum, and also underpins the PBS model.

SPELL stands for:

- STRUCTURE: e.g. having a clear/ supportive routine; avoiding sudden changes to the routine.
- POSITIVE APPROACHES AND EXPECTATIONS: e.g. having realistic expectations or targets; giving lots of encouragement and praise
- EMPATHY: understanding the reasons why someone is upset or angry; that sometimes they resort to challenging behaviour because they are frustrated, and no one is listening to them.
- LOW AROUSAL: e.g. low sensory environments/ not too noisy or crowded
- LINKS: e.g. working in partnership with the individual and other professionals.

# Chapter 4: Active Support

Active Support is about the way we support individuals who receive care and support. Quite often, the priority in the work of health and social care practitioners is to 'keep people safe', and to 'show that you care'. These are natural inclinations and motivations; however Active Support is much more.

Active Support is about seeing the care or support for other individuals, as also a means to help *them* learn or develop skills themselves, to become more involved in their own care and to really experience an enhanced quality of life.

*How does Active Support differ from the hotel model?*

What happens when you go for a stay in a hotel?

- You pay for your service in advance: like a weekend away/ perhaps with breakfast included...!
- You know what you are going to get beforehand
- You hope that the service you get will be 'what it says on the tin'

- The emphasis is upon you as a *customer*. You don't live in the hotel. You wouldn't be welcome going into the kitchen yourself and helping yourself to a midnight feast!
- There are rules you must follow
- The support you receive might not be as flexible as you would like. For example, if you have a disability, they may not have the equipment you need to use their bath facilities.

*How Active Support is different:*

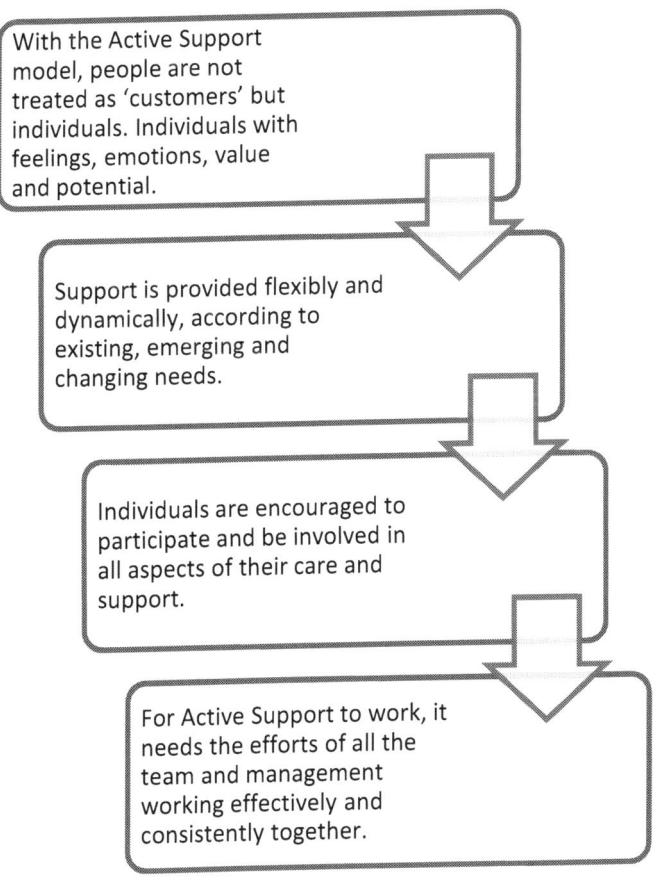

With the Active Support model, people are not treated as 'customers' but individuals. Individuals with feelings, emotions, value and potential.

Support is provided flexibly and dynamically, according to existing, emerging and changing needs.

Individuals are encouraged to participate and be involved in all aspects of their care and support.

For Active Support to work, it needs the efforts of all the team and management working effectively and consistently together.

# The four main principles that underpin Active Support

- Every moment has potential
- Little and often
- Graded assistance
- Maximising choice and control

| Every moment has potential | <ul><li>Individuals who receive care and support can be involved in all aspects of daily living.</li><li>These include everyday activities, such as doing housework, shopping, gardening, visiting friends or relatives.</li><li>All kinds of activities can be seen as opportunities for engagement, learning development and enhancing a person's sense of well-being.</li></ul> |
|---|---|
| Little and often | <ul><li>It takes time to find out an individual's potential. Sometimes,</li></ul> |

| | |
|---|---|
| | this potential will not be noticeable at first, or will develop over time.<br><br>• If introducing a new activity, it is best to only have a go at it for a short time, but not for too long, so the individual can dip in and out, as the relationship and understanding develops between they and the support team. |
| **Graded assistance** | • It's important that staff only provide as much assistance as is required.<br><br>• Too much support can feel 'over-supportive', controlling or restrictive of independence.<br><br>• If too little support is provided, this can lead to the individual failing at an activity and may become put off from trying again. |
| **Maximising choice and control** | • This involves looking out for opportunities all the time: to teach, encourage and develop confidence in individuals, about |

| | the art of making choices and expressing preferences. |
| | • The more frequently their preferences can be responded to, the more likely it is that they will learn that making choices makes sense and will do it more and more. |

## *How to integrate Active Support into everyday practice*

There are three areas where you can integrate Active Support:

- Independence
- Informed Choices
- Quality of life

| Independence | When supporting individuals with their activities, it is important not to give too little or too much support. Too much support, can deprive that individual of an opportunity to learn a skill themselves, or participate in something. Too little, and they might become frustrated, and give up at what they are trying to do. |
|---|---|

There are five levels of support within Active Support. It is important to match what you provide with what the person needs. As a person becomes more familiar with a activity, or more skilled at it, then assistance can be faded out a little.

| | |
|---|---|
| *ASK* | e.g. 'Do you want to take your laundry downstairs now?'; 'Let's take the laundry down now, ok?'. Asking; suggesting or telling. Is just a verbal prompt to tell someone that it's time to do something, or something needs to be done. |
| *INSTRUCT* | e.g. 'Take your laundry downstairs and put by the washing machine'. Instructing someone is useful when the person can do the task physically but needs a little reminder about the steps involved. It does depend on the person's ability to understand instructions, which needs to be simple ideally. |
| *PROMPT* | e.g. Point to the washing machine, and say 'put the laundry in here', or mime putting the washing in. Prompt can be combined with 'instruct'. Prompting is |

| | | useful for people who do not know what to do, but can interpret and follow gestures or signs that point or indicate what they have to do next. |
|---|---|---|
| | *SHOW* | Gives a lot more information than just a prompt. Gives a higher level of support. Involves perhaps a demonstration, and then allowing the other person to do the same thing, or copy. Can be combined with prompt or instruct. E.g. putting some clothes in the washing machine, then giving the person an item of clothing as well, and saying 'like this...' |
| | *GUIDE* | Involves more physical assistance – depending on the person's needs. E.g. guiding someone's hand or arm. |

## Informed Choices

| Person-centred support planning | When a support plan is developed, it should involve the individual, so their wishes and preferences, goals and aspirations, are at its heart. A support plan should also be a living document, and individuals should be supported to ensure it is regularly reviewed, to reflect their changing needs or interest. |
|---|---|
| Communication plan | There should also be a detailed communication plan in place, to enable engagement and communication between staff and the individual. This also helps the individual to be able to express and communicate their choices or preferences. |
| Positive behavioural support plans | Sometimes, an individual will struggle to concentrate for long enough on a task, and may have developed a form of challenging behaviour, as a way to get out of it. |

| | |
|---|---|
| **Opportunities** | Individuals with learning disabilities are often not given opportunities to participate in some activities: although with the right support, they would be able to. Reassuring an individual that they will have the support they need, may encourage them to realise they have a choice whether to take part or not. |

## *Quality of life*

Promoting or enhancing an individual's life involves:

- Supporting them to be part of a community
- Encouraging good relationships with friends and family
- Maintaining relationships that last
- Having opportunities to develop experience and learn new skills
- Having choice and control over life
- Being treated with respect
- Being treated as an individual

## Positive Reinforcement: The importance of praise and encouragement

Giving regular praise and encouragement is very important to encourage individuals to engage and concentrate on new or slightly unfamiliar activities.

Giving praise or encouragement, is sometimes called 'positive reinforcement', because it seeks to encourage individuals to see the connection between a certain activity and what it achieves. Praise helps people to recognise that what they are doing is useful, and that they are doing it well.

Sometimes, the positive reinforcement is naturally reinforcing. For example, if you make a cup of tea – you get to drink it.

You mustn't overuse positive reinforcement, however. If you use positive reinforcement, when an individual already knows how to do an activity well, then the praise will lose its value.

Sometimes when you use praise or positive reinforcement, is just as important as doing it at all. For example, if an individual tries a new activity for the first time, it is important to give praise straight away, and not later after an unreasonable delay, because the individual may not associate the praise with what they did, and it will have lost its sense of value.

Some individuals who have very few skills, or do not participate easily at all, will need a lot more praise than other, perhaps even constant praise.

Different kinds of positive reinforcement work with different people: for example, verbal praise might be valuable to one individual, but not useful to another.

**REFLECTION**

- In what ways could you improve your work practice in terms of implementation of Positive Behavioural Support?
- What aspects of the Active Support model are you carrying out well, and which areas could be improved?
- How could you promote awareness of, and be a champion for the PBS and the Active Support model?

# Conclusion

This book has provided you with an overview of the history of our understanding of autism, and the symptoms and difficulties that affect individuals diagnosed with autism, and their carers. We have also touched on the different reasons and types of challenging behaviour, and strategies to address them. In the third chapter, there was an overview of the principles of Positive Behavioural Support, and in the final chapter we looked more in detail at how model of Active Support can be implemented in practice.

The most important message I would like to end on, is that when supporting individuals with autism, remember that they are unique and precious people: just like you and I.

Retaining that human, compassionate, empathetic outlook, will help you learn how to integrate the theories described in this book, with ease. You will already be half way there.

# References

[i] Wikipedia.org. *John Langdon Down*. [online] Available at: https://en.wikipedia.org/wiki/John_Langdon_Down

[ii] Langdondownmuseum.org.uk. *The History of the Normansfield and Richmond Foundation – Langdon Down Museum*. [online] Available at: https://langdondownmuseum.org.uk/normansfield/the-history-of-the-normansfield-and-richmond-foundation/

[iii] Autismuk.com. *Leo Kanner | Autism independent UK*. [online] Available at: https://www.autismuk.com/home-page/leo-kanner/

[iv] Autism.org.uk. *Sensory differences - National Autistic Society*. [online] Available at: http://www.autism.org.uk/sensory

[v] Autism Speaks. *What Is Asperger Syndrome? | Autism Speaks*. [online] Available at: https://www.autismspeaks.org/family-services/tool-kits/asperger-syndrome-and-high-functioning-autism-tool-kit/how-are-and-hfa-dif

[vi] Ambitious about Autism. *Low functioning, middle functioning, and high functioning Aspergers?*. [online] Available at: https://www.ambitiousaboutautism.org.uk/talk-to-others/2015-04-09/low-functioning-middle-functioning-and-high-functioning-aspergers

[vii] The Autism Families Research Study: Siblings of Children with ASD Research Summary Report Prepared for NAS Cymru by Michael Petalas, Professor Richard Hastings, Dr Susie Nash, and Dr Alan Dowey School of Psychology, Bangor University

[viii] DeWeerdt, S. *Autism characteristics differ by gender, studies find | Spectrum | Autism Research News*. [online] Spectrum | Autism Research News. Available at: https://spectrumnews.org/news/autism-characteristics-differ-by-gender-studies-find/].

[ix] Grinker RR, Yeargin-Allsopp M, & Boyle C (2011) Culture and autism spectrum disorders: the impact on prevalence and recognition. In Autism Spectrum Disorders. D. Amaral, D. Geschwind, and G.Dawson, pp. 112-126. Oxford University Press.

[x] Slade G (2014). Diverse perspectives: the challenges for families affected by autism from black, Asian and minority ethnic communities. London: The National Autistic Society.

[xi] Bankole O (2016). Involving African families in the education of their autistic children. Network Autism

[xii] Alqahtani MM (2012). Understanding autism in Saudi Arabia: A qualitative analysis of the community and cultural context. Journal of Pediatric Neurology; 10(1), 15-22.

[xiii] Papadopulous C (2016). Autism stigma and the role of ethnicity and culture. Network Autism; 1-5

[xiv] Autism.org.uk. *Describing autism - National Autistic Society*. [online] Available at: http://www.autism.org.uk/about/what-is/describing.aspx

[xv] Foundation, T.*What is Challenging Behaviour. Drafts. The Challenging Behaviour Foundation, UK*. [online] Challengingbehaviour.org.uk. Available at: https://www.challengingbehaviour.org.uk/about-us/about-challenging-behaviour/what-is-challenging-behaviour.html

[xvi] Collins S (2010). Supporting Positive Behaviour. A Workbook for Social Care Workers. Jessica Kingsley Publishers; 12-44.

[xvii] BILD, (2014). [online] Available at: https://www.youtube.com/watch?v=WNuW3Xqnjws&feature=youtu.be

[xviii] Autism Speaks. (2018). *Applied Behaviour Analysis (ABA) | Autism Speaks*. [online] Available at: https://www.autismspeaks.org/applied-behavior-analysis-aba-0

[xix] Rcslt.org. [online] Available at: https://www.rcslt.org/speech_and_language_therapy/docs/factsheets/what_is_slt

Printed in Great Britain
by Amazon

59166848R00080